When In Life
Battling With
The Enemy

When In Life Battling With The Enemy

Remember But God

Neveah Torrez

To order additional copies of this book, contact:
Xlibris
844-714-8691
www.Xlibris.com
Orders@Xlibris.com
828201

Intro

I'm Neveah Torrez. I am now 30 years of age my story is to inspire women and young girls also men or young boys all over the world to let them know in life battling with the enemy never give up, never fold as reading my story it will inspire you no matter how hard trials and tribulations are remember but god. I've had to battle a lot of things on my own I had know one in my corner to say "hey", this is happening and here's how you handle it so I'm now telling my story to help those in need those who have lost faith and those who may have gone or going threw similar life crisis that I have experienced. My gift I have is my voice and I'm going to use it to inspire all as we get into the story and always remember "But God".

Life beginnings

Starting life no one tells you how hard or how easy life will be all you know if your born and you have parents to teach or raise you in this world some of anyway but the truth is you are designed to figure out your life path and your to grow into faith and god is to lead you where you need be. Let's get into my story.

I remember growing up as a young girl dreaming I would have the perfect life, perfect parents, my dream car, the best wedding ever, lets just say things didn't go this way life is never perfect you have trials you have tribulations.

(Midland Texas - Mid-Life Crisis)

At the age of 11 my life began to turn all around, My life went into a huge crisis quickly. I walk slowly to the car trying to process what was really going on Desmond was silent the whole way there we get out the car and there is a lady standing there Desmond gets out I begin to see them argue I get out run over and the first words that came out this lady's mouth was "She's not mine she's not even my color" I began to cry and ran to the car I called the mother, I knew and told her I'm coming back home. In my head how can someone who gave birth to you disown you and treat you like that? When I got home I ran to my mother asking what was going on? She began to cry. I sat down. She sat near me and began to tell me my life in the womb up until I was eight months old when she got me. Ashley was her name. I knew the enemy had been in my life since day one. She began to tell me that (Desmond) had been seeing (Amanda) on side and got her pregnant with me and left Amanda end up coming back around telling him she was pregnant and she was also a drug addict to crack cocaine and she was using it with me while she was pregnant. Amanda ended up going into labor. She called Desmond telling him I was a boy and he would be happy and be with her little. Did he know I was a girl? He said he named me Jeremiah on the way to the hospital. He gets there and sees I'm a girl and he leaves this only to make Amanda envious and make the enemy take over and the first eight months of my life Amanda Became more addicted to drugs she then began letting men tamper and molest me and my real sister for drugs. I remember visiting Rebbeca and Kassy and how they would say I remember hearing them play with you little girls using toys and stuff for the drugs but we were all so high on drugs we never cared. As a girl now 12 beginning to see my life hasn't been so perfect at all I feel into rebelliousness, depression, anger like how could three grown women let this happen to me and my sister?. Ashley started telling me that when I was eight months old Amanda put me on a porch and left me there in a shoe box. This lady Ann called them immediately. She said I was all messed up in that area. She had to doctor me and also help me with the shakes at night because I had crack cocaine in my system. She said I wasn't able to have children and that she was sorry this had happened. She never wanted me to find out. As a twelve year old young woman I couldn't understand the story. All I saw was anger and I wanted revenge. How could anyone do this or keep this a secret from a child the enemy wanted me to stray away from birth to his path Desmond would talk about god I would go to church camp but I didn't really know of god? I began to act out skipping school hanging with my step cousins clubbing drinking doing drugs I begin to engage sex at 15 not knowing I had opened the doors for the enemy to plot and lead me in destruction of my life for the next 14 years of my life. No one ever told me in life you have a option to choose life or death the enemy wants you to choose his path I'm telling you choose life because there I was in a storm in my life not caring, not praying I begin going threw tribulation after tribulation suffering being abused in ways I thought was love not know was not love god was the only one who could save love and heal me. My parents no longer mattered to me. I began seeing I was only a meal ticket because Desmond pulled an extra check from the government I had no clue over little did I know it was to support his drug addiction crack cocaine and to spend it on other women.

At the age of eight I started my period you would think this was a good beginning in a little girls mind I wasn't processing this was a blessing with a lesson the enemy thought he had the doctors fully stated I couldn't have children but little did they know "But God" he was fighting battles for me that I was too young to see but as they all say "I once was blind," But now I see, the enemy was now entering my life in all ways. In my mind I was becoming a woman to the enemy; it was opening the gates of hell for him. My periods were bad long very painful. I would throw up, I couldn't walk at times, it had me weakened and to see I would have to experience this once a month in my condition twice a month and it wasn't giving up easily. My parents lacked knowledge in knowing females sometimes need medicine, surgery, and the right obgyn doctor to treat me. I don't blame them on that but this only caused me to suffer for many more years to come. It became part of my life where I ignored it. I was content and in my mind I had to keep pushing regardless this is where I was still under GOD'S wing and though my faith and spirit was low he kept my body covered.

I'm thinking how can I go from a bad situation to something even worse? You guys may see movies like lifetime or Tyler Perry movies not knowing its people out here like me going threw the exact same issues in real life. The movie Cinderella I lived that I was in a two parent home dad gone all the time. My step-mom was sick on and off I had two step sisters a step brother but I was always the outcast. I had to raise myself and teach myself about life and others. I was a step child but also a slave in their eyes. I was to keep the house clean very clean. My mother cooked and I was to do all household chores. Maria who was out of the house. Sierra, very envious and a very evil Chad who hated the fact Ashley took me in at birth. I knew I had a long road ahead of me. So many days I couldn't understand my life was I put here to suffer all my life? Tyler Perry movies I lived between the battle of domestic violence relationships, health, narcissistic lovers, drug abuse, mental and verbal abuse I was living in the world of sin and the path of enemy which caused me tribulations that I wasn't supposed to walk and I had no understanding what I was doing but on the inside it felt good it felt like I was on top of the world but in reality with what I know now I was basically giving my life the enemy which caused me to suffer in life longer than I was supposed to I lived in that life fifteen years. I began turning to the street life because I figured the people I was meeting had my back and I become a coldhearted savage teenager that didn't care about anything or anyone. I started dressing provocative drinking, doing Ecstasy, weed, cocaine, anything that had me thinking I was no longer in pain and that my life was ok. But I started opening doors that know one could close but me and god.

At the age fifteen, I thought I found love I meet a guy name Albert at first, things were ok he was nineteen going on twenty I was still a sophomore in high school and seen him as all that the popular girls had older boyfriends who would pick them up for lunch and buy them gifts I was now popular living the club life still doing drugs and now I had an older guy and to me that's all I needed. As I said before this was a door that should have been closed. As things got serious for me and Albert so did my life. God had already given me a warning before destruction and I missed it. I remember going to the library to get books. I picked up two books out of nowhere and my teacher walked behind me and said "Neveah if I didn't know any better Are you pregnant and getting beat? I replied, "No I just wanted to read about this now I'm fifteen what made these books catch my eye out of all the books in the library? It was a sign from god and I missed the entire clue. After the first year in the relationship one day I found myself behind two trash cans in Albert's car getting beat up for the first time in my life because I wouldn't give him my paycheck now my first thought was am I supposed to be in this? What happened? I'm very loyal, I work, go to school. Why was he doing this to me? He dropped me off. I ran into the house straight to my room. I broke down crying. I could begin feeling my face swell my lip busted blood everywhere I got strength enough to clean myself and prepare for when my parents came home and how they would react. My mom walked in. I began to paste back and forth. What do I say? Do I lie? My mom walks in my room hey "chilli " that was a nickname she gave me. I turned around and she began to scream what happened? I told her I got jumped by some girls at school. I was ok but I was suspended for three days. She was like oh my gosh I need to call the school I told her it was ok they would leave a voicemail. How stupid was I to lie for this man that just beat me like this? She believed me and walked out the room. Albert was blowing up the phone trying to explain himself and tell me I just need to listen and he loves me this will never happen again. As a young woman now sixteen I thought ok he's right he won't do it again he loves me but looking back as a grown woman now that isn't love, love is patience and not easily angered like God.

I found myself now being beat, verbal abuse, and mentally abused on a daily the enemy has seen a door open and is using this opportunity to stay under his wing. I still found ways to party with my cousins and go to clubs under him I tried talking to other guys but nothing ever worked I felt trapped with this guy. I start coming home with more black eyes and busted lips my parent's finally figured out what was going on as a mother she tried giving me advice here and there and I remember my dad saying "don't help help her she will figure out she will get tired" what type of parent says that? What type of parent sit back and let there child get beat regardless of the situation in my mind I'm crying for help I need a way out why are my parents letting this happen to me? I begin to dislike them and thought hey they don't care why should I he beats me but he's the only one really showing me love I started not care either and it became something I was use to in my life black eyes were ok to me my nose swollen was ok to me him pulling my hair out was ok to me him humiliating me in front of others slapping me making me pull my clothes down to smell my underwear taking my pay check to help him sell drugs spitting on me calling me names hurting me from the top of my body to the inside was all ok to me when in reality it wasn't no man should hit a woman no man should embarrass his girlfriend no man should think it's ok to tell a woman he just beat to lay down and let's make love this is all the enemy but I was too blind to see. I turn seventeen he has a hold on me still I decide to wake up one day and move out with him and his mom little did I know this was the gates of hell for me. More beatings occurred more control was given I was to go to school work and hang with his mom and sister. I came home one day, after school and he must have just did some cocaine his eyes were fiery red I walk in an he immediately attacked me his mom standing over me watching I'm at a cry for help his sister finally start helping when these things occurred but that day she was almost a bit late I get up when she gets him off of me and my face big as a balloon my nose swelling were it was hard to breathe his mom walk besides me and says well start listening to your man do what your suppose to do and this wouldn't happen? A grown woman sitting back watching her son beat me to pulse was ok in her eyes. I was surrounded by nothing but evil half of my life and I didn't understand. They leave and leave me there with him I was laying down with ice on my face and he enters the room and tells me he's sorry now its time for me to have sex with him lady's regardless of the fact when a man beats you and turn around for you to have sex that's rape so not only was I in this life of pure hell getting beat and manipulated I was a rape victim once again. He did this all the time like it was making up for his wrong doing and I accepted it. Now at seventeen still going to school working I joined a program called CIS (Community in schools) it helped you with future goals school work going to college, I remember going on a high school trip to visit colleges though my life was a mess I still had goals in life I picked TWU in Denton, Texas it was a nursing school I was happy though I have not talked to my parents I know they would be glad but shortly my life was to change again. I get back from the trip I get sick I'm cramping really bad I call to Albert to take to the hospital he tells me to walk so I walk to the hospital so sick not understanding what was wrong I get in they draw blood plug me to an I.V. and I'm so scared the doctor walk in "How old are you? I say," I'm 17 and will be eighteen next month, he replies, "Well from the blood work you're two weeks pregnant I'm like "no I can't have kids. He's like well you're pregnant. I started crying I haven't talked to my parents since I moved out I call them and of course they say

"How dumb are you there goes your career and hung up in my face I heard my step sister Maria laughing in the background so I'm walking back to Albertmom house flustered angry like why me I was now a young teenage girl getting beat, basically homeless, no car, now pregnant and I have to go home and face him. I get into the house. I call everyone to the living room. I tell them "I'm pregnant" they all seem to be happy he was jumping up in joy so I thought maybe things would change and they would only get worse. Desmond calls me two weeks later and tells me to meet up with him so I went alone he tells me it's time to level up in life I needed to get myself together I cry and cry he looks down at me with disgust I tell him to help me get an apartment I think he doesn't hear me but a month later after my birthday witch now eighteen I have my own apartment I'm still going to school working carrying my unborn child still trying to maintain and focus. Albert didn't let me go alone this was a way out that god had given me and I invited the enemy right back in now I'm getting beat while pregnant I begin to hate myself I begin to think I was dumb and no longer needed to be on earth but I had sense enough to know my child needed me as a mother. I finally stood up to him I was about seven months pregnant he comes home one late night and I have school in the morning I was now going to a alternative school since it was my senior year and I was pregnant they had a bus to pick me up and bring me home I knew the bus came at 6:00 am to get me he came in about 5:30 am so I was already up getting ready for school he, "says were you going? I say, "to school" he says your not going you need to have sex with me before you go I told him I had no time the bus was coming he walked behind me and pushed me on the cabinet I remember hitting my head and it begun to bleed he threw me on the bed I was going in and out of consciousness to cope with him I started crying yelling for him to get off me the bus had pulled up waiting on me and I told him I had to go he gets mad and as I'm getting up to go he pushes me and I fall right on my stomach I felt my baby move I began crying harder I knew I had to get up I ran to the bus head still bleeding I'm holding my stomach hoping my baby was ok I see the bus monitor running to help me she called the police and they would meet us at the school I was tired of this mess I was tired of being a victim the police came and always I told them I was fine I just wanted my parent's I missed all my classes that day my parent's came screaming saying I had to move back home and they were going to help me for the first time in my life I was getting help. I was so happy to go check on my baby and go get my things from the apartment. Little did I know this would start a HATE war between me and him. I was happy though I was finally in my own room getting spoiled due to my baby. I was going to school still working. I was proud of myself but the enemy doesn't want you to be happy. I graduated 8 months pregnant two months early and at the top of my class yes I still got my diploma it was a goal for me and I did it. Desmond decides to help me throw my baby shower and we will see what the baby was back then. We had no gender reveal parties. It was all old school me having the heart I have. I invited him and family though I had not spoken with them since I moved out of the apartment with him. So we all show up happy Desmond is making food I go on to tell them that its a BOY and I was naming him Isiah Paul Brown he was originally due June 19th of 2008 everyone cheered but here comes the enemy Albert finally showed up with rage in his eyes he walk to get a plate of food his mother told him the news he gets angry you not naming him after me I said no you beat me almost killed my child and tell people it's not yours I sure am not oh he didn't like I now had a voice of my own he walk up to me and smashes the plate of food in my face everyone is furious but does nothing I began to walk to Desmond's car in pain, hurt embarrassment here I was again going threw abuse in public my dad drove me home I didn't talk to him the whole way because once again you didn't stand up for me. Well time goes by and my doctor ask me if I want to be induced I say yes I was tired of being pregnant and I wanted to meet my son so June 9th of 2008 I had walked in to deliver my baby I had to be there at 5am oh when I get there his mom him his sister are greeting me at the door I had no time for drama I was about to become a mother. As we all no we couldn't have a lot of people in the room Albert was getting upset and begin to argue with me my blood pressure got sky high my dad steps in they begin to argue then my mom begins to argue with his mom wow all because my baby the nurses and doctor kicked Albert and Jenny out told them they had to wait outside the waiting room oh boy he is mad but they were making me stress and my baby was stressing too he brought that on himself he sends a text telling me when he sees me I would get my butt beat for disrespecting him but I paid him no mind. My son finally came weighing six pounds and 19 inches Christ says, "he not mine he's not even my color ring a bell my son was already living a generational curse that I was living and, I said he's yours I'm light but no need to argue his mother that's probably; "her dad's baby or the mailman like lady are you still being cruel after all this I told them to get a DNA test and that was that. We get the DNA oh its 99% his they were shocked I had to prove my son was his for them to come around. I began to cry like how could a young woman who was told they couldn't bare children have such a pretty little boy he was so little very light complected like me but from the abuse and me not knowing real love I went into post par-tum with him I didn't want to hold him or be around him all I had in my mind was he was of his father and I didn't want to be apart but my mom stepped in and helped me with him she feed him, spoiled him, babysat him while I went to work life was going good I started actually learning on my own to love, nurture, protect, hold and give him the love I never had the enemy wasn't just on my life he wanted my baby as well. My life was so horrible, no real family members on my side, no real friends. All I saw was disaster but I had to keep going. I remember not hearing from Albert or seeing him after that I mean I was happy I wasn't get abused anymore but this turned on my innocent child abandonment from his father because I wouldn't be with him I knew as a young teen parent I had to keep going regardless no one in my ear but that's why I say remember "But GOD" he had already made me a strong enough woman to live I just needed to find my purpose. Albert calls me one day, hey, I have a room you should come you and the baby so we can make this right I told him I would let him see his son but I was no longer involved with him he acted like he understood little did I no I was walking back in the gates of hell I went to the room sat there it took him almost 2 hours to get there now that I look back god was sending me a sign to leave then. He gets there I'm up making a bottle for my baby he walks in puts a chair behind the door and started beating me I was yelling no one came he broke my cell phone I had no were to run I see my son playing on the bed with blood everywhere not even saying why he's mad he begin to choke me I begin to blackout from the hits and the choking I remember something telling me to tell him I'm sorry I yelled "I'm sorry" and he lets me go I see my son milk all over the place blood everywhere he yells clean this up and get yourself together I need sex now like in my mind did I get myself back in this situation I clean the blood and try to ice my face I lay down and gives him what he wants not to stare up any trouble. I told him after I needed to go my baby had no milk but he refused to let me leave luckily my mom had made him a cereal bottle and I knew that would hold him until checkout time I'm looking in the mirror walking around the room and I'm just heartless I had two black eyes one know on my temple my nose felt broke my ribs were bruised he sat back in joy looking at me but little did he know this was the last time he would see me and my baby I woke up every hour waiting on check out time 12 came and I hopped up well I gotta go he needs milk and I gotta get home he was like I'm paying for another day I was so furious but god didn't let him have enough money to get another day. I was happy I walked to my car told him I would contact him when I get home I got in the car and cried I cried hard I drove to my associate friends Lisa house because I knew my parents would be furious her mom ran to get my baby told me to go the hospital and she had my son I go they tell me I'm bleeding on the inside of my face as well the call the police once again I tell them I'm good this time I knew for sure I wasn't going back. I go grab my son I start to head home and I see my mom and dad outside I pull up and they are angry yelling at me asking my would I let this happen I was only letting him see his son days went by he started riding by the house I had a new phone but he couldn't contact me this lead him to pulling up on me everywhere I went like how could he know were I was I remember him saying, "I smell your scent so I don't need your phone that was very sickening. A month passed by I meant I wasn't going back I wanted better for me and my son and he couldn't be apart of it well god seen I was trying he sent me peace out of nowhere I got phone call saying Albert had been picked up by the Us marshals and there was no telling when he would get out I jumped for joy and cried because he wasn't going to leave me alone. Now still eighteen no baby father around my mind immediately went into club mode I had not had a teenage life because I was fifteen and stayed with him until I was eighteen and I needed to party but god didn't send me peace to go back in disaster but I didn't care I was young and ready to get out there opening more evil doors to my life.

With Albert now gone I got me a new apartment, a new car, a decent job I was now taking care of my business but as I always say the enemy always snuck back in to get me distracted from my calling. I turned into a woman that was very dangerous I turned into a bitter mad hurt young woman. I was clubbing Monday thru Saturday I had a somewhat type of relationship with Albert mom so my son was there most of the time when I started partying I changed my whole mind frame I what I mean by that is the somewhat information I would get from Desmond witch he raised me into as woman with a man's mindset plus the street life have gave me more knowledge about life the wrong life but oh boy this was not good I begun doing guys how they would do women and I didn't care what the street life labeled me I thought I was the female of the world guys wanted me left and right but to talk to me it was like a job application you had to be semi qualified and if I accepted you. You were now a groupie to me and there was a time for promotion if needed. I felt I was the star in Midland, Texas I then began a crew called Kit Kat Krew guys new us for wearing the shortest shorts showing cleavage and my crew could dance so in the club we took over. I'm drinking out this world doing drugs again this was life but in reality it wasn't this had opened more trials and tribulations in my life more than what I knew. I got so good at what I did I started to think more like a man and became the leader of the group I had girls in my corner following me around basically worshiping the ground I stepped on I then started to pimp them I seen this was a way for me to gain more street creed and become a real "G" in the streets I had lost track of my life I've always made sure I keep a roof over my head food on the table a decent car but now that I was in the pimp game I had to level up and get nice things these girls made money for me and them I treated them different then the other pimps on the street I made sure they had money a place to say food I didn't beat them I supplied them with the drugs they needed I was breaking them down and building them up faster then what I knew this caused me to hate wars with the guys I was a intimidating woman that had power to do what they did and they couldn't stand it I found myself arguing and in drama with more guys in my life then females but this my world my way and either you got with it or got lost. I was living the best life as they say to have groupies guys who knew about each other and knew it was only me they answered too and females selling their body for me was so gut reaching to me I stood in this world like I was God but oh no with every enemy choice you make there is a consequence and I would reek what I sow very soon. I wasn't into relationships because I wanted more than one guy. I had a Monday guy Wednesday guy Friday and the weekend was for me. I had to travel to take my girls to our clients. I had no room for distraction. I became greedy. I just didn't have the girls working for me. I had a part time job and I also got into the drug game selling pills for Desmond. oh this was lovely more money flowing in more than I could imagine I know your thinking how did I gain a relationship with Desmond well he was the enemy and it is the fact that I was doing what he did lead him to respect me in this type of matter I was helping him organize the females he had then we went into competition funny. I thought this life I was living was all that I needed no one could tell me anything so god started putting me through my tribulations. I'm now twenty one years of age living good. I remember one of my girls started having trouble with one of the guys she had kids with. We went out to the club one day. We saw him. We think nothing of it. She knows she is safe with me and I wasn't letting anyone touch my girls. Well the next morning I get up were about to head to do a call I start my car and it shuts off I'm like I know I have enough gas to make it to the store my top girl (Sierra) starts to scream" look your gas cap is broke off something is leaking I got out the car I seen a bottle of castor oil by the tire lets just say they guy that we seen wanted her so bad but I wouldn't let him have her he put castor oil in my gas tank witch caused my engine to shut down I was angry I started to cry I needed my car that was my money I called desmond he was pissed we had just both signed on this brand new 2008 Chevy aveo and before our eyes knew it was gone. He came racing over and we had it towed the guy had to pay for the damages but they couldn't get the oil out. It was cool I got money but I can't go to the car lot so we bought just a little bucket off the streets so I could get back to business. I wasn't letting anything stop me. The club was my life I would still go see my son and take him what he needed but I was on a mission God decided to try to turn me around once again with the lifestyle I was living I could of easily been someone's cell mate that why I say as you read and look at my life remember "But God". In between this time Ashley had gotten very sick she had stomach cancer I remember her telling us then she went straight to hospice after thirty days she passed away so fast I was living this life and she was dying the whole time I began self hate guilt even though she wasn't the best of mom to me I felt a type of way. In the bible it says, "you aren't supposed to love your parents more than you yourself" I never really knew what was love was anyway I just cared a lot but this had me mad I started getting into the street more I picked up a few more girls in my mind my heart was to hurt others but in reality your supposed to "love thy neighbors as god loves you". I didn't have any understanding of that because the enemy had me so cold hearted I seen nothing but me. God was keeping me from behind those prison walls and I thank him for that. I turn 22 still living my best life only to be snapped back into reality soon I end up meeting a guy named (Issac) he had just got out of jail and he was digging your girl. We became attached but he had to realize the life I was living he accepted it and came around when he was supposed too. I was still doing my thing. I had meet a new groupie and he was the top one so most of the time I was with him. I remember having this period app on my phone to keep up with my monthly periods and after my son I wanted no more kids. I had no time. I got up one morning and my top girl says dang "Mama" your boobs getting huge I laughed it off like yea I no let's get our day started but then my period app popped up on my phone two days late I was like oh late she was like you pregnant I was like nah after five years I can't have no more kids girl so we laughed it off little did I no I would have change my lifestyle very quickly. I ended up going to the doctor and they did a pregnancy test and sonogram for some reason and there I was pregnant again at the age of twenty two going on twenty three years of age. I was so devastated I had to change my life up quickly. I started saying I didn't want my baby adoption was good but something in me wouldn't let that happen. I had this baby on the way. I had too tell my girls I was done with them I let the top girl take over I stopped selling drugs I told my groupies they had to go I was about to become a mom again and my baby needed me. I had to re-adjust my life with a baby on the way I remember going to get my son so he was home with me I stopped going to the club I would go every so often I started working at a daycare were me and son would go together I wasn't on any drugs me and the guy Issac decided to be together even though he knew the baby wasn't his I now started living a normal life I know your thinking how could I just change my life again I say "But God" he made me and he made my mind he knew I was strong he knew I could do anything I put my mind to. But I want you to keep this in mind the life that I choose to live before my baby girl it just didn't go away I had consequences that I had to go threw. Me and Issac were doing ok we knew we had a baby coming and we had to keep it together well I start getting very sick with my baby I was so snappy Issac decided to leave me so here I was a young woman single now a single mom of what was about to be two kids they guy I got pregnant from had a whole nother life so that left me with my baby on my own but I still had to maintain for them. I got the doctor and they do a sonogram. Its a Girl I was excited. I had named her Diamond Marie Wilson her original date was August 11 the day of my sister's birthday. It was a blessing again I was having kids and I wasn't even supposed to bare any this was a blessing. I remained very sick with my little girl I ended up with Pre-clampsia and super high blood pressure my hands and feet would swell real bad I was still all alone I was coldhearted so I had cut everyone off when my mom passed Desmond moved to Kentucky so I was really all alone but I was stubborn and didn't care. I end up going to a specialist because the doctor I had act like he couldn't figure out there was something wrong with me the specialist says maam we have to do a emergency c section now she's only two pounds she not getting any oxygen or food your placenta had start shutting down he says I don't know how she's even alive you have to go to Odessa, Texas now. I was furious oh my gosh how could this be happening I cried I called Desmond he got in the car doing 100 mph he said from Kentucky I called Albert mom to help me pack and get ready I let her take my son and take my car because there was know telling when I would get out, this was too much I was no longer having extra money come in I had a real job and if your not there you don't get paid but I couldn't worry I had to get this baby out I arrive at the hospital and I'm scared I don't know what to think at this point I had no one with me at the time until Brittany showed up they said emergency c-section but they took three days to do it. I went in on a Tuesday and Thursday night my doctor came and started the process. They took five times to get my epidural in my back I remember him cutting my stomach open and feeling everything I grabbed hold of the bars that were on side of me and took all the pain for them to get my baby out that man was of the enemy if I knew back then I would have got a new doctor well thirty minutes into the surgery I hear "CODE RED" security Desmond was drunk when he got to the hospital and start talking crap to the nurses because he heard them over talking about how many times the anistelogist poked me in my back, but out comes my baby I hear no cry no scream she's purple and blue, I look towards Nicole and asked if she died? My looked at me with buck eyes and put her head down remember I knew of god but I wasn't praying like I should I begin feeling them stich me up and I started to cry doctors were moving so fast with my little girl I was furious then I heard her cry as they stuck the tube down her throat I was overjoyed at the last minute the doctor gave me something under my nose that I smelled and passed out from I wake up in my room sore this is my first c-section my son I pushed out so this feeling was different I can say I would push out a baby any day. The nurse walks in and says if you want to see your baby you have to get up and walk remind I was so in pain I barley seen the color of my baby girl and what she looked like so I got up holding my stomach and I walked and walked till I couldn't walk anymore I walk to the N.I.C.U. and I had no clue of how to take care of NICU babies I just knew I had to level up in life and get ready for my to come home. I walk in and wash up you had scrub up every time they were very strict there I walk to my baby girl and she's laying there with tubes she so small my baby girl had to get three blood transfusions a pick line her feeding tube but she was a fighter she was almost on room air even though she was low of blood, oxygen, he left lung was collapsed, she had stomach deflation, she was allergic to milk so had to quit pumping she was alimentium for her source of milk she was also battling sleep apnea she was on caffeine drops and also had asthma so oh boy I tell you this was an assignment for me. At the age of twenty three without Ashley and Desmond back in Kentucky I was clueless but I was determined to take care of my baby the enemy was on my baby's life and she was giving up Diamond actually means rhythm and she moves and fights for her life. I began battling with the enemy in the NICU some of the nurses treated my baby unfair wouldn't seek to her proper needs or anything I got very ugly with a few people in there about my baby I'm not play when it comes to my babies or my innocent little girl who didn't ask to be here four months went by I finally get the call and they tell me she's about ready to come home and I needed to take the parent class and car seat class for her while she was in there that gave me a little time to get my one bedroom apartment together for her, me, my son, and Issac he had come back and I was so blessed with that. I'm still at this daycare and I tell my manager I had to take off to get my baby and I remember sitting down with her and her sister and there crying telling me that they would help me and I had open doors little did I know this was enemy once again. Me and Albert's mom go to get my baby that Friday I took her clothes and shoes I was dressing my princess up like her mama she was a diva in my eyes I dressed her got her ready we waited like two hours before they even brought her back but they had to do last minute testing to do on her I was anxious I knew, "mom reality hit when I put her in her car seat and put her in the car Albert's mom sat in the back with her we had a few people coming by to see her so we rushed back home. Me and Issac had started our lives he stepped up as a father and help me with her I still worked at the daycare so me getting up at eight was a hassle but we rotated getting up changing pampers, giving medicine, feeding her all the above until I got her a spot in the daycare were I worked. Issac keep my son home with, so I didn't have to worry about him. My manager finally got her spot and she started at the day care.Her and (Sammy) came up to me and said they would start right away helping me with her I jumped right on it me and Issac were tired and needed help. On down for a few months I began seeing CPS (Child Protective Services) and police in my life like crazy these people I worked for seen this as an opportunity to try to take my baby but I wasn't playing about my baby I was a good mom I wasn't on any drugs we may have had a one bedroom but I was doing what it takes to take care of my kids. They started coming by drug testing me and Issac and I remember one day being very irate with the lady and she broke down and told me they were trying to take my baby but if that was to happen then my sister would get my baby girl so I don't know why they thought they could I pulled up on them me and Issac and got the rest of my baby girls things they were heated I told her no maam if you weren't lien to your husband about having kids you wouldn't be sick in the head to steal someone's else's she her sister Sammy was the bribe person she said she would help me but in reality she up and moved and left with her sister and husband for help but hey were so sick mined they wanted my baby girl the enemy was on me bad "But God" The CPS lady finally closed all the cases I had ... I had a case that they said I was medical negligence to my baby girl they tried to say Issac burned my baby with cigarette's I mean these people were sick never again would I open the door for someone to help with my kids if it wasn't me and Issac it was no body. Me and Issac weren't on good terms either four years into our relationship and we were arguing more fighting we begin being roommate's at this point my baby girl was walking she was about two years old now between her doctor's appointment I still maintained a part time job for income she stayed with Issac I babied him so he sat at home and took care of the kids while I worked but I was about feed up a man should help provide for the family I start showing him he needed to work and regardless if you loose a job get another one but things were still rocky the enemy wasn't done. We were know in our two bedroom two bath I was happy but the office staff and maintenance people were always on me and Issac. I was still happy I had graduated from Midland College and I had my pharmacy technician license and I had got us a brand-new jeep Cherokee remind you the enemy wasn't done with me yet. I remember Issac getting into it with the maintenance people so bad we got kicked out she didn't like me any way for some reason I would go to the office for extra days for my rent and should laugh in my face telling me oh since your crying I'm supposed to feel sorry for you hahaha I never understood why people would be so mean to me but when you have a calling on your life others can see that and they don't like it because they see it I never knew my calling until later on with my life but I was tired of the crap. Issac got into it with them one day so bad they kicked us out I remember I was furious I had never been in this situation before Brittany offered to help take care my son he was still in school and me, my baby girl and Issac would go to Big Spring, Texas to live with his mom. I mean out of town? A new city? I had to suck it up I was losing everything right in front of my eyes my apartment, my jeep, my job, my luck was now at rock bottom but the way god built me I had to stand on my two feet this wasn't stopping me. I was now twenty-four with two kids and I had to figure of a way to get us out of this mess we were in.

(Big Spring, Texas - Life or Death)

So here we were moving my things to Big Spring, Texas I was sad I had to leave my son behind, but he needed to finish school. Me and Issac started working at buffalo wild wings in Midland and his mom would watch my baby girl while we worked biggest mistake in my life she had diaper rashes and was always moody I then found a girl named Tisha stayed there in Big Spring too so got in contact with her I started taking my baby there she had four girls so I knew my baby would be ok there. I remember Tisha calling me and I got back in for work and she was like let me show you around lets go out I hop in the shower go out Issac watches Diamond we go from bar to bar and I remember her walking up to a guy in the bar for a cigarette and he comes over we begin to hit it off immediately I know what you're thinking Issac was at home, but me and him had grew out of love we were together because my little girl knew him as dad and we trying to do good but I meet this guy (Tyrone) is what they called him on the streets little did I know this was the first time I actually knew I was dealing with a narrsatic and I ignored all red flags. Well I go back home a couple weeks later me and Tyrone began hanging talking on the phone it was great to me Issac really showed no interest in like he cared anyway. One day getting back from work we show up the police is there well his mom didn't tell us she was behind on rent they gave us two weeks to get out I mean again the enemy keep trying to break me so here I was stressing about finding a house for us. I called in between when we were at work or when we got on the highway everyday to drive back home from Midland. I finally find us a two bedroom trailer house far but it was a place to call home his mom couldn't get a place in Big Spring if you leave as a bad tenant they have a blacklist and if your name is seen on that from other landlords they will not take you in so she had to move all her stuff in my kids room and they stayed in the living room. Well before I knew it the month was coming up to pay rent and all of a sudden the car I had start acting up I was missing work then out of the blue me and Issac get into it and he gets up the next morning and says "Well I don't know what your going to do I'm leaving" I'm like what his mom pulls up in a U-Haul to load there stuff lets not forget the day before were she wouldn't take us back too Big Spring because I wouldn't give them a key to my door she me and Issac had to come up with gad money to go back home and I had my baby girl with me you see how people do you when you try to be nice this whole time I never knew why people treated me the way they did but when God's light in you others can see that and they will stop anything for you not to shine. I'm so blessed we made it back home that night so when they took off to leave that was a load off my shoulder I had took care a grown man for four almost five years even though he did purpose once during our relationship it wasn't going to make anything better. Well with the enemy on me knowing how strong I am my daughter that day started running behind him and she fell and broke her arm I thought she had just fell but she had broken her arm I had to get her in a cast that next week so now I was twenty four my son was still with my sister, my car was breaking down, I had to find another place to move too, I had lost my job my life was falling all apart again "But God" I end up moving in with Tisha I'm not the type of person to stay with anyone so I jumped in on finding me another job I stacked up money for another car I found a lady selling a car in Odessa Texas, for a thousand dollars and we spoke she let me do half and half so picked up another car I had me a job I went to then begin looking for houses a lady called me back with a two bedroom one bath for six fifty I took it I gave her the rest of the money I had and moved in that day Tisha and her husband were surprised within the two months I stayed there I made a way for me and kids no help no family to open there arms they all left me high and dry waiting on me to fail I even called me dad and he had no care in the world "But God", me and my little girl pack up quickly she is so happy I finally have my son's aunt drive him from Midland to Big Spring so he could come home I was getting my life back but remember the devil hates the strong you have in you. I meet a guy named Jeremy around this time I had started talking back to Tryone too so I was really happy I had everything back and I had two guy friends to talk too well me and jeremy hit it off K2 decided to get him a girlfriend too so everything was all ok Jeremy was a guy you thought you wanted he was a big time drug dealer he paid all the bills helped me with my kids I only paid the cell phone bill he was very charming but also twofaced he would switch sides all the time and start drama between every person I would talk too even my homegirls I began to talk too but I loved him so know one could tell me about him he had me so fooled was was cheating on me the whole time Jeremy did cocaine really bad and I started back doing it with him I never knew that if a person could take you back to your past you don't need them I was blind and couldn't see I was having a blast but the enemy was just beginning with me again. With my kids in school me working part time me and Mario began to fade away with each other I end up finding out that he was cheating on me, so I left him. Me and Tryone linked back up he still had his girlfriend and we decided to be friends and no too long we began being intimate with each other he became being controlling didn't want me talking to other guys if he even heard a guy was talking to me in the bar he would correct them and remind you he has a girlfriend he would tell me that he would beat on her from time to time but she was a cocaine addict and like alcohol so she started the fights most of the time me not being smart I don't know why I thought he wouldn't do it to me. I'm also now battling with my health again I got my tubes tied and after that my periods were worse than before I was pretty much use to that though but now the doctors included my blood pressure and diabetes was starting to look a little bad desmond has it and my grandpa died from it but I wasn't taking it serious at the time. The enemy was attacking me all ways currently. Jeremy end up coming back around so I wanted to go back to him I told tyrone and that night he pulled up and came to my house with a car full guys to fight jeremy and jeremy had just got out the hospital but he had no choice to fight I got in the middle and told them they better not jump him I would fight too so I stood in the middle and let them fight Jeremy beat him up and they left tyrone tried to choke me but Jeremy got right in the middle to stop him. Tryone blew up my phone all night my kids were sleeping so they didn't see any of this thank god. Me and Jeremy continued to be together well Jeremy has to go out of town one weekend I had start hanging with this girl Rissa so I was at her house on weekends well tyrone called me and we were arguing back and forth I told him I didn't have to listen to him and I no longer wanted to be with him well he pulls up to where I am him and his friend and I was now in a fight I was getting jumped by two guys I turn to fight the other guy and when I turned back around tyrone hit me so hard in my eye he broke my eye socket I feel to the ground remind you the girl never grabbed my kids I was getting jumped and my kids were victims of this I remember I'm on the ground and he still hits me over and over I feel the other guy kicking me and punching my ribs if my son would have not ran outside and yelled "get off my mom" there is no telling what would of happened they ran and speed off in the car I thought the girl Rissa was calling the police she called Tyrones current girlfriend to me it sounded like a set up I could me eye swelling shut I threw up I was in pain so bad my son that was ten at the time helped me the car and I drove home I ran to my room crying like how could I let myself get in this mess I called Jeremy he was on his way back speeding from Lubbock Texas he got there and broke down he wanted to hurt Tyrone he said well Jeremy leaves and I don't hear from him again now I was all alone in this my kids had school the next day and I put a shirt over my eye I had to walk my daughter in school she was only in head start it was so embarrassing to walk around like that the teacher asked was I ok I told her yes and ran off. I went to the hospital as soon as I walk in the doors close behind me I hear "Code Red" a lady grabs me quickly into a room the next five minutes came and I had dozed off I woke up to six police officers in my face taking pictures and asking me questions let me remind you guys I had traffic tickets but I didn't think of anything at that time in my mind I knew the police was on my side and I had nothing to worry about but the enemy had plans. They asked me what happened, who had did it, I was scared to tell them but I did anyways the nurses rush in and say they have to open my eye to make sure nothing was broke 3 nurses held me down and I screamed it hurt so bad to open my eye they took xrays and everything thirty minutes into the ER visit they tell me he broke my eye it was a orbital eye fracture he had hit me so hard me left eye dropped in my socket, along with a fractured nose bruised ribs, at twenty eight years old how did I find myself back in this situation? They said I needed to see a plastic surgeon for my face here I was now a single mom two kids a somewhat steady income I was in the process of moving to another house in Big Spring now another victim to domestic violence and added I had to see a plastic surgeon. I tell people all the time there is a God because with all this how am I still sane? How am I still pushing? I know by now a person would be in a metal institution, jail, drugs, anything and I wasn't I knew I still had kids to take care of. Well lets say the enemy had more for me. I go home after the hospital and I get my lids from school we eat, shower, and lay down. The next morning comes I'm in so much pain my eye is throbbing I get up to take my kids to school and I come back home to clean I hear a knock on my door its the police I'm happy I'm like they found him everything is good he says "Neveah looks like your eye is a little better, I reply, Yes sir its hurting but I'm OK." He says well I see I have a few warrants for you your gonna have to come with me. My heart starts pounding I'm like what? My kids are at school I have no one to get them and I know my traffic tickets were not that serious he says well they want ya come on. I'm pissed now I was the victim how could I get beat up and now going to jail when the guy that did this is out there free? It made no sense I called Desmond to rush here to get my children oh boy the enemy had me trapped in all ways Desmond said he was on the way and I went to jail with my eye broken I was crying I couldn't understand what was going on I had to move I didn't have time for this. Well we get to the jail I was so embarrassed everyone thought the police had beat me. I'm in there a whole day before I see the judge I walk in to talk to him his face and eyes got blurry he almost broke down He tells me "Neveah I pray for you and whoever did that needs to face consequences I'm giving you time served. I began to cry and told him thank you but the enemy was right there I go back outside to wait to be released two hours go by I ask what's going on somehow there is new charge of theft I'm like what? Desmond was paying for beds for my kids threw rent a center and had stop paying they waited till the balance went up and pressed charges you guys I can't make this up here I was walking to my freedom just to get put back in a cell I began to panic my kids are home I have to move I have to get my deposit everything was falling in front of my face again. I called Desmond and got on to him he said he forgot and I told him to tell the people to pick the stuff up and I'll be free of the charges. Well he does that they come get the items but now it was up to them to go to the court and stop the charges this lady took another two days to drop chargers I'm now in here for three days wondering about my kids. All the things I had to do I had no more time to wait I start calling my so called friends to help no one could help my dad couldn't even help I start calling bail bondsman for help it was 500$ to get my out I had no money I end up calling a guy that was at a bail bonds company and he keep asking do you have anyone to help? I gave him the numbers of the people I knew I called him back and he says no one wants to help you I began to cry I need to get out of here. A few hours later they tell me to get up I as bonded out the lady from Aaron had called and said she would go the next business day but the guy I talked to the bondsman place came and got me I was so happy I keep telling him thank you he told me he felt bad because none of those people wanted to help me it was like God had touched him to come get me I told him I would pay him back when I got the money he told me it was fine don't worry about it I felt relived little did I know the enemy was still attacking me I get home my kids run outside to me happy, they both say mom papa let the water get cut off and he said the lights were almost off like I just got out of one situation to come home to this? I immediate start going off on him he says he had no money but my son told me he had a pocket full I told him to leave not only did he sit back and let my water get cut off, or almost let my lights get cut off the whole time I was in jail he was tampering (touching) on my daughter yes that's right something had he ask my children it was on my conscious and I be darn he was touching on my little girl. Now lets re cap this again here I am a single mother twenty eight years old with two kids no help from there dads, another victim of domestic violence, I just got out of jail, I have to move, my lights are almost off, my water is off, and now my daughter was touched while i was gone But remember but god, at this time I was seeing no way out I was on the verge of a mental breakdown, but in my mind I had no time for that I went off on Desmond he tells me he thinks he might of touched her when putting her in the tub like are you serious I call the police and report it guess what its still under investigation and its 2020 but people think the system cares oh really? Well I put that in gods hand I had to do a miracle in two days I call the light company to extend my lights they help me out also transfer my lights to my new place, I call the water company and she helps me out and turns my water back on and also helps me transfer my service. God was helping me despite of what the enemy thought he had planned. In the process of me moving the new place lets me pay my deposit out with my rent I was back on top during this time I was healing myself and also having to heal my daughter letting her no nothing was her fault pray and I'll never leave her side again. I told her god will take care of them i knew then i had to heal so i could heal my daughter. You guys this was so tough for me because I already experienced that growing up and I didn't want my children to go threw that but here we were. I started feeling self guilt, self hate, but remember in life the enemy wants your mind im here to tell you keep fighting every battle is different but keep fighting and believing god will help you and see you threw if you haven't realized by now he does send angels to help you in the midst of our storms. I know a lot of you are like how can I believe there is a god? All I can say is my entire life is a blessing I know he's real because look at my life the enemy is trying to tear me apart but god is by my side he's the only one his grace the holy-spirit it was pushes me everyday I believe one day my pain, my suffering, will double as he says in the bible I have no doubt one day all this will be behind me and I will live in the blessing he has for me. So we move in our new place and for some reason I no its not home for me what I meant was I had a feeling I wouldn't be there long but to make the best of it. Months go by and everything is OK but in life stuff is only perfect for so long well one day I get up to take my kids to school I get pulled over the guy us the enemy right off the back he tells me to get out I'm asking him what's the reason he doesn't have on he twist my wrist in front of my kids throwing me on the car I'm applaud, like here we go again were in this church parking lot and I'm looking up like gods help me its freezing outside he had my hands twisted up my kids are crying in the back seat, I see another car pull up he must been on god side he tells the guy to release me and send me on my way. They guy wasn't hearing it he said my license was suspended and I was going to jail if I didn't call someone to get them (CPS) will get them I can't believe this happening I forgot to renew my license and he could of gave me a warning and I had no one to call to get my kids at the time. I started crying the other police officer yelled "let her go just give her a ticket". He was pissed he let me go the other officer drove off I told him thank you but the other officer wasn't finished he walks up to my car in rage throwing five tickets for stuff he made up I was like this is crazy. My kids went back home with me for that day they had seen to much and needed to rest up. The next day I take my kids to school I stop by the court house to see how I could take care of it the same judge who let me go also was in charge of tickets he told me I could do community service and that would pay for them I was happy because I knew a lady at the salvation army and I knew she would help me. The next early morning I get up to renew my license online and start my community hours I had no time for work luckily when I moved I got accepted for housing so my rent wasn't a lot an that was a blessing, and if your wondering the cops still haven't found Tyrone it had been six months and my eye was healed but I still avoiding the plastic eye surgeon. But I go to the salvation army I had 70 hours to do but with god grace the lady signed all my hours and I promised her I would stop by everyday to talk to her this was a blessing because I needed to start work. So months go by and I'm back working a part time job my kids are in school I'm doing ok I began to start back talking to guys but nothing to serious yet because of the situation that had happened but of course my calling in life must me huge here comes the enemy once again. I found out Tyrone had moved two streets behind me with his girlfriend and he had been watching my every move. One day coming home my car began to smoke I get home to see what's going on and I have a oil leak like OK I just got my life back on track here we go again. My neighbor said I would be OK it was small but we go to the store and car ripped in flames the fire fighters had to come put it out here I was car less again like how could my life be so harsh. But god made me who I am for a reason I don't dwell on what's going on I make something happen. Luckily my job understood and told me to come back when I got transportation luckily I had been putting money back I go on Facebook to a group of people who sell used cars for good prices I end up talking to a lady in Odessa and she had a Camry for 1500 I told her I would bring 850$ and do the rest in payments she agreed so she brought it to me and let me do payments with the rest I was so happy we had a car again. I know your wondering how am I still making it I can't say anything but god, My birthday comes around I'm now twenty nine my kids are nine and four time flies by so fast well remember I said K2 had moved two streets behind me he began driving by, knocking on my door, I was under a protective order with victim services and I called and told her what was going on she told to me hold out they would get him soon. So I was just avoiding it at the time the enemy seen I had help so he sends me someone to remind me he's still around I had been talking to guy named Matt on this dating website for months I told him I was taking things slow so we were just talking we decided to finally meet each other and Matt was forty with three sons and a single father he had a good job very easy going I thought this was a breakthrough boy was I was wrong. I know you're wondering why keep going in and out of relationships but i was lost broken and looking for love. Matt came over he showed up in a red suit with flowers and chocolate he swept me off my feet or could I say I was gullible, but does that ring a bell red suite and flowers? The enemy shows up in any form or fashion and knows the bible very good I didn't know that information but I do now. This would be the first time I ran into someone that was a Narcissistic these people are dangerous and very charming its crazy because as me and him are dating now I didn't see any signs but I remember I would see a guy on a video from my Facebook everyday talking about narcissistic people and I had no idea that was my sign from god to run. I had feel head over heels for this guy our kids had finally meet we are living like we would have a family soon. His kids were nice I had stopped working he was paying my bills I was relaxing but little did I know the enemy had it out for me once again. Well months go by and me him are planning to have, my tubes reversed and to move in with him as a woman I never moved in with guy I hate taught myself to always keep my own. Well I pack up a few things for me and my kids and slightly move back to Midland Texas I had withdrew them from school and they were now in Midland district things were moving so fast I had forgot about my real life but luckily I keep my house and still paid rent on it. One day Matt gets a phone call and his bestfriend daughter had got shot in the head and they were planning her funeral as his women I felt like I needed to support him and go with him so that next weekend we were going to Dallas Texas for a funeral. The week comes up we leave the kids at home his oldest son was seventeen so we were good with the kids being home. Some reason I start getting sick, throwing up not feeling to good but I went anyway to be honest I believe god did that so I wouldn't go. I keep missing signs from him. Well we are on the road to Dallas I book our room and we are headed that way I mean we were in good spirits I remember him saying on the way there his best friend and another guy friend we were going to see tried talking to his last girlfriend and it was drama but they were back friends I told him he didn't have to worry about that I would tell him if someone was trying to hit on me he said OK, and we left it like that. We show up I'm really not talking because I didn't no these people and they were meeting me on the day of a funeral so I felt out of place anyway well with Narcissist people they don't care about anyone feelings but there's and they love center of attention. I noticed Edward starting to get jealous because everyone was admiring the fact I was cuter than his last girlfriend so I started to open up slowly like I was in the family. He didn't like that at all. But the next day we get up to go to The funereal I cried like it was my own child and Matt keep looking across at me like if he could yell shut up he would. That's when I knew something wasn't right. The funeral ended we are now lead into the church to eat with the family we sit down to eat everyone is eager to know who I am I stood up to shake hands and talk to them Matts best friend comes over to shake my hand and introduce himself I tell him I'm sorry for his loss and we start talking about what his baby girl was like when she was here I end up getting a phone call and I go outside a old high-school friend Stephanie seen I was in Dallas and wanted me to stop by I see Matt rushing to the car I hung with Stephanie he gets in the car and says "Neveah don't make me tear this church up, I seen him holding your hand to much don't make me act up" I say that's your best friend his daughter just died why would you think its something else? He says "You heard what I said. I got to thinking this is a second red flag for me. I remember Matt saying he was into different spiritual belief's but I was a fool in Christ and had know understanding this was about to be a huge wake up call for me. So the day goes on me and Matt go out to eat then we proceed and go to The Improve Comedy Show this was my first time I was happy, Matt began to change in public he was acting loud looking at women in front me and heads up ladies God doesn't send someone to you with wondering eyes. I looked passed it were laughing the show he kept getting phone calls from his other friend to show up to a party for his son I told Matt we can go for a little bit and little did I know were in a building that the Mason actually worshiped in. We get there and were having fun I step outside with his friend to smoke remind you I haven't smoked marijuana in while so were outside smoking and talking I see Matt walk out to the car with three cups I thought nothing of it I go back inside Matt says are you drinking tonight? I reply a little bit not a lot for all my woman watch your surroundings and were you go and always make your own drinks. Matt comes over and gives me the first cup I take two big gulps and I say "I don't want this its too strong, he takes the cup goes to make me another drink buy this moment I'm feeling good I smoked so I'm just vibing to the music he comes back gives me the second drink and after I take that one sip my head start spinning and I see black I fall to the ground not realizing what is going on I hear my body drop and I fall unconsciousness I feel someone shaking me but I can't get up I try opening my eyes and its a blur he's over me yelling my name and I see his face but its a dark shadow the enemy was trying to take my life I have no energy to move three people from the party lifted me on a chair but this was different my throat felt like it was closing my heart felt like it was about to explode I hear a lady say "call the ambulance" Matt says "no take her to the car she will be OK. I'm blacking in and out at this moment trying to remain calm so I could have a little airway to breathe we hit the highway to the hospital I'm freaking out because I can't understand what is going on? Edward says "I seen two disrespectful things that happened last night that won't happen again. I began to cry slowly still trying to breathe the best way I know how now realizing Matt set me up out of jealousy and tried killing me I go back unconscious I wake up and I'm in the hospital an IV in my arm and a EKG on my heart I try to sit up Matt is sitting in the chairs across from me with a range of anger his eyes were red he says 'Calm down I guess you actually might make it" I'm thinking like what but it wasn't over I flat line on the table this as the first time I was experiencing a outer body experience I hear the bells going off the nurses rushing in to clamp my heart on the machine I could see everything but I couldn't feel it I was standing above them watching them work on me I can't make this up Matt is still sitting there with rage I began to feel my eyes close and now there is a light I was in a dark room with a light I could hear footsteps pacing back and forth like it was god trying to decide to take me now or let me live I slowly start feeling my spirit fade away my eyes began to close and I say I repent and I'm sorry almost a minute away from dieing I hear the door close and light fade away I then hopped back in my body and woke up with a deep breathe like I was being suffocated, I felt my veins flowing back with blood I see my feet go from purple back to normal I snatch the oxygen and put it in my nose. My god wasn't done with me yet I began to yell at the doctors for not trying to help me, and to treat what was going on with my body but they looked like they didn't believe me because Matt had told them another story but "GOD" I instantly tell them to take all the stuff off me I was getting up to use the bathroom they removed everything and with my strength I get up I look back and oh boy Matt looked pissed. They release me but don't tell me a diganios we get back to the room

Edward is speechless I tell him I'm tired I'm going to sleep. The enmeny wasn't done. The next morning we were about to get up Matt was up before me I see him putting the bags in the car so we could head back to Midland and get to the kids Matt is asking me questions and I can't reply I woke up to find out I have no voice and I couldn't walk I start crying what is going on with my body I'm useless I can't talk, walk, I have to get to my kids Matt is smirking like I can't see him I'm still so blind by the red flags and the enemy. Matt is more irritated now that he has to pack me around we get in the car and the whole four hours back to Midland the ride was silent we pull up at home and my kids are the first to notice like what happened Matt is now jolly telling them I got a little sick not worry I head towards the room to lay down I have no energy to eat or drink at this time. Edward takes the kids out he said I needed rest so I went to sleep. Matt comes back with the kids he says its raining and cold outside I in my mind I was like oh OK? I ask Matt to help me up so I could shower he says' Neveah I'm going to be honest it doesn't look like you will make it threw this it feels like you are a burden to me "I began to cry he says' you and you kids have to go now. I'm appalled I struggle to talk and ask him really he nods his head remind you the kids are bed sleep for school tomorrow somehow I get strength enough to get up start getting my things and waking my kids up all the kids got up like what's going on I tell my kids come on we have to go I remember my son crying he was like I prayed for a dad and brother what happened he says mom you can hardly walk and talk what's going on? I tell him just come on we have to go struggling to get to my car its raining we finally get in the car a tad bit wet and I go to start my car, it won't start I was like oh my god, I prayed for god to help me I told him I wouldn't come back here just please help me something says 'start your car" I started my car and it turned on with barely any energy in my legs I start to drive its cold, wet, rainy, dark I can hardly see at night but god had me Big Spring was thirty minutes away and I knew I had to get my kids home. We arrive home my son helps me and we go in the house mi glad I had common sense enough to keep paying rent on my house we get settled in and the next morning I get a call from Dallas hospital saying that my blood came back positive for a

GHB a date rape drug and methamphetamine I was like I dot do drugs the doctor says I know he says who ever did this knew you would have a reaction to it and they wanted you heart to explode in your sleep. All I could do was cry and think why? Me why do I have to keep going threw these things in life? I was walking myself right into death because I was walking with the enemy and not god but God was still there holding on to my life at that moment I knew I had to change my life I had to start walking back with Christ and leaving everything to Christ this was a good thing for me but the enemy I was betraying him and I wasn't going to like him it didn't matter because I almost lost my life in Dallas and left my kids behind I had to stand firm in my decision and not look back. I bet your wondering if I called the police of course I did this happened in 2018 and its 2020 guess what there still investigating. I end up calling a step family member Taylor she had already been threw what I been threw and was already a sister in Christ she began to pray over me and says God will help you figure it out. Another month goes by I had to teach myself to walk and talk again. It was like I was a baby I made sure my kids didn't have to worry I tend to keep my health to myself because there my kids and need to live life. It came to me that since I had choose life it was time for me go from Big Spring I was stuck because I just signed a new lease and I had to wait but God he puts it on me to check back with victim services and tell them Tyrone was harassing me I needed to relocate I told her that and the lady says "Neveah I'm giving you sixty days to relocate I'm typing a letter for you to break your lease so you can go your kids deserve more "I was shocked this happened so quickly but I knew I was dedicated to get it done with my kids back in school I had plenty time. I go pick up the letter I take it to my landlord she's mad but under the Violence Against Women Act they had know choice I wasn't just street smart I'm book smart too and I know my laws please educate yourself. So it began I had sixty days to go from Big Spring. I didn't know were to go but it came to me Abilene it was one hour and thirty minutes away but it was enough for me. *I began going to Abilene, Texas to start putting in applications and deposits for a place may I remind you if its God will he will open doors and resources for you to move I had little money but what I did have I had to make what was best. God put it on my heart to call the old church I went to I called her and asked for help she pledged half of my deposit for us to move in I was so grateful after the phone call with her the apartments called back and said I was approved things were going perfect so I typed up my sixty day notice and I call to rent a uhal truck an I start packing up. I was shocked still that I was moving again with me and my kids but I knew god had us. The day finally comes I withdraw my kids again and we began loading the truck the lady from victim services helps us pack and get loaded she and her husband drove the truck we cleaned the house back up I drive fast to drop off my keys we stop by the store to grab snacks get gas and head out I remember telling my kids this is our new beginning in life we will be OK remember never get comfortable anywhere it may be a time god will have to make you uncomfortable to leave never get constant unless its his plan to have you in the place your in. We head off the highway I put Abilene Texas in my GPS and we hit the highway we started driving and tears were just flowing I was proud of myself being as strong as I am to make things happen and get us out of where we were. In hear to say we are all blind once in our lives are we are all fools to Christ once in our life but I'm telling you know never give up keep fighting walk with Christ everyday you have the choice to either decide Life or Death every morning choose Life god will make sure his angles are there to protect you but do know the more you get with Christ the harder the battles are but don't be afraid that is only the enemy God will lead you threw just keep faith, sometimes when don't praise or worship him he still has his arm in the way of the enemy not to touch you be grateful of the things you have in life and most of all be grateful to live another day. Me and my kids were our way to a new beginning but the enemy once again was not done with me my calling and gift that god gave me is a huge testimony and the enemy doesn't want me to walk with Christ but what he doesn't know is the harder he comes for me the harder my fight and love goes towards Christ life is a battle daily you go threw things ... You will experience battles that your not sure your going to make it I'm, hear to tell you Remember But God he will help you every-step of the way I was a beginner back at Christ but I was eager to learn our lives our in the bible spiritual awakening is good to have people think life is ran off days life is ran off time that's so the father above can give us messages we need with time. We finally make it to Abilene I swear the drive said an hour and thirty minutes with my music on I got there in less than an hour it felt like I had drove so fast I lost the uhaual truck and had to call them to give directions. I know your wondering was I scared to be in a new place, know friends, know family, I wasn't Big Spring was the same way I had to figure out my life and I wasn't alone God was with me. The lady finally pulls up and we start unloading we get what we took I gave her a hug told her thank you she told me that she loved me and to be careful. It didn't hit me that I was actually in a new town until she drove off but that was the day I knew I had better plans in life and I had to focus to get to them. My kids were excited we were very happy bit again as I always say the enemy only lets you be happy for so long he will come again and oh boy Abilene wasn't what I thought. It would be this town was going to make me strong, new, aware, and even stronger in Christ.*

Abilene Texas, (Growth)

So here I was in Abilene Texas, it wasn't new to me it kicked in that I was alone but I had to began my new life the enemy was still on me even though I had started new life. I had got my kids registered for school we were learning our area around we began going to the mall going to do family things coming from Big Spring Abilene looked like a city to us we could actually get out the house and breathe a little. Things were going good I even started as a leasing agent at a apartment complex life was great two months starting in and I began to battle with my health all over again remind you as long as I ran the streets and gave joy to the enemy I didnt have to worry about my health but when you start to transition things get harder I began going to the doctor every two weeks I'm now twenty nine years old battling blood pressure problems again, border line pre-diabetic, vitamin D deficiency, and Andomyosis (occurs when the tissue grows into the muscular walls of the uterus) (enlarged uterus and heavy periods) I didn't understand were all this had came from I was now in a new battle with the enemy I thought can I just catch a break?. One day I started bleeding from two days in between months at a time this was making me miss work a lot I was sick all the time I was very worried I would think about if I pass away who would get my kids? Who would take care my babies? That was a reason for me to fight everyday. March rolls around and I'm in the hospital I'm in surgery getting a DNC (remove tissue from inside the uterus) (to scrape the uterine wall) because my pap smear should my lining was to thick and needed to be scraped in order to bleed properly.

I was upset this was painful it was like having another kid brittany came down for the surgery and I had a guy friend Chris go come over to help assist me for a few days luckily I was strong enough I still had to take my kids to school and pick them up sore and all that's what sucks about not having a support system I took things in my own hands and this time the enemy really got involved. I had been talking to a guy named Calvin we were old high school friends and we crushed on each other nothing too serious just conversation he stayed in big spring so he knew of the complication I was going threw. Months after the surgery I began to bleed everyday all day non stop I found my doctors putting me on pills every two weeks to stop my bleeding the surgery only irradiated what I had I found myself were I had lost my job into only because if the illness but as I was leveling up in life and didn't know it people really treated me wrong at jib places because of the knowledge I had the light of Christ burning in me and a glow that intimidated anyone. I was a fool in Christ still and didn't know I had a bright future ahead me I just needed to stay focused on the right path I was OK as far as a job because I was on housing but not just regular housing I was in the FSS (Family Self-Sufficiency) program with housing this was a program that helped you get off of housing every month when I pay my rent they match the rent I pay and out it into an escrow account and after 5 years they would give you the money saved up and give it to you to buy a house cash with this is a resource every single mother needs to take advantage of to help them in life. So rent was taken care of and I had extra income coming in to help with bills this was a blessing in itself to be honest. September comes and I'm still bleeding the doctor I was seeing wanted to do an Ablation (a procedure that surgically destroys the lining of your uterus). I said no the guy was really just doing procedures collecting money off my insurance I had at the time prior to this I seen a doctor from San Angelo Texas before I left Big Spring and he said I would have to have a Hysterectomy (a procedure to remove a woman's uterus) I cried and told him no as well I wanted one more baby and I never called him again. Here I was lost wondering what to do I was at a mental breakdown and didn't no what to do. I keep trying to work past the bleeding but it only got worst I end up somehow talking to guy I had meet threw Tisha remind yourself again with every blessing there is A Battle the enemy knew I was close to a breakthrough and wanted to interfere again. This guy I had known from Midland were were cool but we never seen each other like that. As weeks go by I called the doctor in San Angelo he says "Neveah I've been waiting on you are you ready for your Hysterectomy? I replied NO but I'm ready to be normal again I'm tired of the pain I'm tired of the bleeding. He told me to call first thing that Monday and he will get it scheduled. I sat and cried this was a huge decision I was making but not only was I worried about that who was going to keep, my kids and take them to school? San Angelo was and hour and 30 minutes away I was furious but god had fixed it prior to this I was still working I started going back to church and one day I told my pastor I was going into surgery and I would be out a few months that next day he had his help schedule me food deliveries for when I got back home, a church member signed up to help watch my kids for the two or three days I was in San Angelo he also had me gift cards sent to my home for me and my kids this was a blessing now that was out the way I needed someone at home with me for a few days so I ask Tisha and the guy Calvin if they would come help me and they both said yes my sister and my niece said they would come by for the surgery but had to go afterwards mi glad I had some type of support. My surgery date was October 2 2019 it seemed like when he set that date stuff started happening I start bleeding more I was really sick I was at work for the last day before my surgery and I began to hurt this felt like labor pains I began to cry and I ran to the bathroom I get in the bathroom and something tells me to push I began pushing and a huge circle like object came out I took a picture sent it to brittany she says that's a miscarriage I'm like no way my tubes are tied funny thing is I had been bleeding none stop and all my Abilene doctor would do is subscribe me medicine when in reality I was having a tubal pregnancy this whole time I could of died with the baby sitting in my tubes "BUT GOD" I tell my manager I have to go I head to the hospital and there think I'm making it up I told the man I have noticed my boobs were leaking milk but I thought nothing of it. Luckily by the grace of god I passed all I needed when I pushed the baby out because they weren't trying to help me in any kind of way they enemy was trying to plot in any way. I felt bad but I had to keep going I had no time to dwell on what happened I had to get ready for my surgery since I didn't react the enemy was mad he was plotting something heavy for me since I had won that battle. So here the day comes and I'm up getting ready to go to San Angelo for my surgery I tell my kids I love them and I'll see them in a few days things were all set I had picked up tisha and Calvin from Big Spring the night before I had no time to be on the highway like that. We arrive and brittany and mariah meet us there we are waiting on a room. They get me back and start my IV they tell my guest to wait in the waiting room as I'm going up the nurse says Are you guys going to give her HUG? Mariah comes over Tisha and brittany don't even bother to move this showed me then there was there jealousy and hate why? I needed this done I had to have it done I wouldn't have any more children and I would no longer have periods you would think they would be happy the enemy was upset obviously. The procedure is done I wake up they began to make me walk to get me moving the next day I was going home to start recovery at home. brittany and mariah had left Tisha and Calvin were still there with me. I'm released and on my home the next day, I get home and the church has meal prepared people are stopping by to check on me I'm slowly healing four days go by and Tisha has to get back home so I tell Calvin to take her home and take my son so she could get home. Now still recovering with Calvin still there to help he was helping with my kids, bathing me, fixing the food, answering the door, cleaning I thought this was perfect oh boy did the enemy have another plot. One day I was up moving slowly and we needed to do, laundry I tell my kids to get there stuff ready we had enough cash but I tell Calvin to take the car? and go get? we go to coin machine was broke. He tells me OK I'll be right back. Hours pass I had something on my mind I'm calling him no answer, phone going to voice mail I ask this house of a friends he may be at well he's not there one of his family members she calls me right away and says she will have her mom call me a hour passes by and I answer its Calvins mom she says, is this Neveah? ma'am she says, honey I'm so sorry I just got word Ronny took your car to Dallas? dropped what do you mean my car is another city

Dallas Texas was? from Abilene I? crying I told her I just had surgery, that is my only car, my kids have to get? appointment, also needed to grocery shop like how could someone take a single mothers car? I'm a new town no friends, or family this was messed up I couldn't believe? this I was in pain still? too be a dream. I call the police out to take a report and report my car stolen well by law? I gave him the keys I had to wait 48 hrs until they put it out for stolen in the system. My heart was? everywhere I had no money, no one to help me my sister never came to assist me. Sparkle didn't have a car but she wasn't any help either how was I going to get threw this? Seems like everyone I had partially in my corner was waiting on my down fall but little did they know God had been calling me home and when I started going back to church I re dedicated my life and soul to him and I was praying and believing in him. Funny thing is when I pray I also pray for protection over my? car and also, the whole world who has a cars everything needs protection. Keep in mind everything was in my car my purse all the information you never think it could happen to you I'm hear I tell you think again I had to call around the car oil places to get my vin number and license plate number I didn't know any of? it I never cared to either well I had to get on it if they were going to find my car. I end up getting the information I needed so Dallas could start looking Dallas is a very big city and I was furious about them finding it there is no telling were he would be. I keep calling Calvin no answer I'm furious days go by nothing they finally put it in the system as stolen and I had to have faith and wait my mind was reminding me that police take up to years to find cars sometimes its never found. His mom called me the next day and gives me an address on were my car may be and tells me again she was sorry, Calvin had been on meth for a few years and this wasn't the first time he did something like this he took his last girlfriends car and sold it for drugs I told her I had no clue he was in drugs but I pray he didn't sell my car for drugs I call Dallas to give them the location she gave me and let them handle it well not enough stress I'm still recovering from my surgery with no help the church stop answering me like I was putting stress on there life but the enemy was upset I choose life and was on me hard on top of that my 30th birthday was a few weeks I had a planned a skate party seemed like stuff was going down hill once again I'm still praying and crying at night tossing and turning I get a phone call on a Sunday at 12 am I hear an officer say We have apprehended the car and he is arrested and you can pick up your car in downtown Dallas I was happy but I had no money and no way there. This was a blessing they found my car within two weeks this was abnormal to me I was shocked but I believed and keep faith god had me and my kids. With push comes to shove I call Desmond I haven't talked to him since the Big Spring issue happened but in the bible it says one day your same enemy will be of help and a resource to you, treat others how you want to be treated this was a hard pill for me to swallow but god told me everything will be OK I knew mentally I had to move different and cordial with him. I call him and tells him what happens he was sad and began to say what I could do I was on top of it but I needed him to come take me and also put money in when we go it was a good thing they found the car but you know the government wants his share my car was 500$ to get out it was 25$ a day to sit there I had to wait another week until I had my portion so that's why they price was so high the enemy was on me and I still stood tall. Desmond and katie was coming to my house for the first time I had to break down to my daughter she was OK I had her back it wouldn't happen again to forgive and pray for him he was only going to be there two days and she would sleep in my room with me with the door locked the bathroom was in my room so she was OK. My head was spinning but I had to get our car. He comes and immediately notices I am different the enemy is in him and I can see it he's like oh your not going to the club? Oh your not going to a friends house? You don't have a dude that your going to see? I start laughing never entertain the enemy I was like no I'm at home working and taking care my kids the streets are no longer for me the streets don't love nobody. He's shocked I'm like yea I'm going in my room I'll see you in the am I really had no words to say to him a person that doesn't see that's there's not something wrong with there character will never change love those people from a distance. Me and my daughter and son enjoyed a movie night and good rest Desmond was irritated that he couldn't no longer destroy my life I was once a fool in Christ but now

I was wise with understanding and God gave me my third eye. We are about to leave he notices I have on clothes he's like oh your not wearing those little clothes anymore I said no I'm not trashy I'm now classy I won't find the right husband dressed in that attire he was puzzled I grinned and went to the car the ride to Dallas was silent he was still trying to process when god pulled me out of the fire and gave me wisdom we get there and we get my car I'm happy its still one piece I was so blessed my purse with all my identification and credit cards were still in there Calvin was driving around in my car with all my items in a trash bag and my daughters car seat was in the trunk I was so happy I got my car we begin to drive back I tell him he can head home I was good and I appreciate it he put his down and drove on I was standing firm on my word my little girl was my precious baby and god was now head of our household. With things trying to go back normal I was still trying to process the surgery from my body I was now 30 years old with a hysterectomy. I began working again and everything was fine you would think I would stop talking to men but that's one thing the enemy knows when your not healed from something the enemy will repeatably send it again and again to see how much he can brake you though I was in Christ I beginning to do self love it important the way things work is that you love god, you love yourself, than that teaches you to love others the enemy didn't like this I was soon to be tested again. I thought Abilene was a fresh start the whole time for me it was a Growth process. I began chatting with a guy named Scott I meet on Facebook things were OK a few months later we decided to meet up I had it bad with bringing people in my home because sometimes I wanted to be comfortable in my own home biggest mistake when meeting someone go to a public place never exchange address's. Here it was Christmas day a ex church member invited me over to her house with my kids and I asked if he could take along we get there and stuff is going great but this would be a night I would never forget. My phone rings and its a girlfriend of mine video chatting were talking laughing I looked over at him and his eyes were full if rage we began to pack up I go outside and he come behind me give me your phone your on phone restriction I was like I'm grown don't tell me he snatches my phone we get in the car he begins to argue I tell him don't do that in front of my kids we get to my apartment and my kids go to there room and he still down to argue saying I was flirting with the girl on the phone he was jealous and then he says it don't matter get her down here because you and her will sell your body for me. Sound familiar this is why I say watch what you do to people because it can easily turn on you I had lust for a (romantic pimp) this was what they were doing now since it got harder to sell women they were pretending to love women get in really good mess with there minds and trick them into selling there body I have never ran into this it was new to me because I had gave up that lifestyle years ago but it tried to come back and haunt me I'm glad I re gave my life to Christ so that he could make me aware in the world Generational curses are also real just like Karma. I told him no I use to sell women why would I sell myself he had an addiction for drugs but I wasn't going to be his drug ticket I go to the closet to change he walks behind me and begins to choke me I start crying my head is like RED FLAG flight mode I yanked away from him I knew I'd severed better I ran to get my kids and told them to go for help they run to my maintenance man apartment for help I grab my keys and phone he tackles me he squeezing my hand so hard he's breaking my nails I yell for him to let me go he grabs my keys and my phone I run out the door were my kids are the police is on the way Scott decides to take my phone and car here I was again back in the same situation like god just got me my car back I have no time to worry I'm just glad were OK we go back home and my kids lay down I go back to the neighbors to use there phone so I can call someone I call my sister and her response was they always whopping on you that's crazy hope y'all are OK like what kind of advice was that you weren't going to come help me or give me encouraging words this was when I knew I really had no one in my corner for help but God that was when I decided I had to let my sister go she was letting the enemy control her life and was jealousy and envy of me. I go back home and about 3 o'clock I hear a boom on my door its Scott he tells me my car was at sonic and if I called the police back he would go get it in my head I was happy god was in the midst of this storm with me and because I had enough self love to no that guy wasn't for me it was a level up for me in life I was learning to love myself I was learning my self worth I knew I needed someone that loved me just like god and if they didn't I had a choice not to talk to them you can become choosy when you want the right person for you but sometimes even rejecting a guy can cause issues I never understood. Ladies you do have a voice know your self worth. He gives me back my phone and says "I've spared you your car, your phone, and half of your life what will you give me? The enemy was all in this man if you ever had someone say I slept next to the devil I have encountered him numerous of times and I'm glad my armor is on with Christ I told him nothing now get my car I'll call tell them that you brought it back and that it he agreed but I knew he had something up his sleeve. He returns my car thank god and he says well I'm gone I won't be back I was like OK great I'll call the police and you have a good day. I can't make this up as write this book I read over my chapters and really can't believe how bad the enemy was really on my life. Two weeks go by and one day I'm walking in the house I get threatening text message that says your lucky you had your kids with you I had some females who were going to ride down on you today but you will make money for me one way or another. I was sick to my stomach he was watching my apartment I had to do something I go to the police station and let me just tell you the Police Department doesn't care about crime I show to press charges Scott already had a third degree felony because they said he strangled me in my apartment I show the guy the text messages he says well that's not bad he's only called five times and texts you three times I have cases here that go threw more than that in my head I'm like really this is why women die all over the world because we show up for help and we get a negative police officer who doesn't care I asked to speak with the Lieutenant how could someone say that the enemy was still plotting on me the lieutenant acted like he cared and said they would take care of it and he was sorry about the officer. I didn't stop there I had victim services type me a letter so I could move the housing authority started Turing they back on me they act like they didn't want to help but I was going to make it regardless god had me. I decided to move across town but the apartment wouldn't be ready in time so I end up transferring to a town house in the same apartment complex I was no scared I gave all my problems to god and I wasn't worried about Scott no longer. The town house was what I wanted anyway it was a fight and battle to get it the enemy doesn't want you having anything but I got it so we are now in a 3 bedroom two bathroom house up stairs down stairs it was nice some may think this was nothing but it was everything to me and my kids they were up stairs and I was down stairs but I knew Abilene wasn't the place for me I was only in Abilene to grow and level up in life not to make it my home. I began getting more with Christ I had began talking to Taylor again and she was a backbone for me because she had already gave her life to Christ a few years back so with me beginning she was helping me fully I no longer had fear, worry, anxiety, she talked me threw the process of re loving god giving my life to him and believing in my heart he would heal and provide my needs it wasn't hard for me because I knew god had been waiting on me. I began to think different, see different, hear different, I was know seeing the energy of people I count see before god was showing me I was no longer blind and Christ and to trust him. I believe that because how am I still standing? How am I not on drugs? How was I changing my life from the wicked ways to good? Nobody but god how was my body healing on a daily from hurt, pain, sorrow? By now if you weren't believing in Christ as your reading my book you should now I'm a walking testimony as I write this book the enemy is still attacking me because he knows my book is going to change life's for ever my book was my voice which the enemy had been trying to steal, kill, and destroy for years but when god says yes nobody can take that from you. Taylor told me one day do you ever look up the town that your staying in and I said no she says Abilene Texas in the bible means growth I was shocked but interested I said OK will do from here on out and as so you all that's how I got my chapters Midland Texas in the bible meant (Mid- Life Crisis) as you read that was exactly what happened Big Spring Texas in the bible means (Life or Death) and remember I almost died twice it actually happened and now Abilene Texas has taught me nothing but growth my attitude has changed, the way I dress has changed, the way I handle situations have changed I finally figured out I didn't have to be in rage or evil my weapon was my melody threw Christ the way I start teaching my kids were different break the generational curses teach your kids what you were not taught so they no how to live in today's world. Also I no a lot of you are thinking how could someone who has battled all this and still battling still have joy, peace, love and believe god? I don't question him as I look back god tried to call me to him along time ago but I keep hitting my head entertaining the enemy but now I walk with Christ in me I'm not perfect god still is fixing me but always remember to cherish life because the next person may be going threw worse than what you are. So months are going away and I'm starting to change I also learned sometimes god lets the enemy take you back to levels in life to see if you have faith to keep going with Christ or do you flee and return to the enemy your past sometimes comes back into your life for a distraction have self-awareness and remember sometimes if the enemy can't get to you he will use family member's, friends, and even your own children to find a way in keep faith and keep fighting. The enemy was so mad at me he tried to take my son out I get a call one day from the school and they say your son has been stabbed in the neck with a pencil. I run to the school how could this happen? Is he OK? What was going on? I remained calm and my son ran to me he told me there was a race war in PE. a fight broke out and he had to fight and the little boy stabbed my son in the neck my mind went to prison like he was in jail schools were no longer safe these people didn't care they wouldn't release his name and sent him to a DAEP school for detention said I couldn't press charges because my son was the aggressor really how odd is that? I'm glad I pray for my children and I'm glad god blocked that pencil going threw his neck I was so angry and I wanted revenge god said let it go I got it and as hard as that has been for me I gave it to god and I told my son too forgive the boy and pray for him. I'm just glad my son was OK. Again as I write this book I'm still battling but I'm still holding on to my faith. Now a few weeks after that I start noticing body pain body aches I felt more of this after I had my surgery I was soon to find out now at 30 years of age along with my other health issues I have Fibromayglyia (a diagnosis of body chronic pain) (its comes from stress, trauma, abuse, emotional stress, I never knew all these years I was holding my burdens for so long it was beginning to affect my body. Lets re-cap I'm now 30 years old with high-blood pressure, pre diabetic, vitamin D deficient, lactose intolerant now also due to multiple stomach surgeries, and now Fibomayglia I can't make this up but you know what since I've giving my life back to Christ and really gave god all my burdens I'm not worried with what there trying to diagnosis me with god said give it all to me and not worry and that's exactly what I'm doing I believe in my heart he will heal and fix me in due time I have to be patience and also obedient threw Christ. The enemy is still on my life today but I walk by faith not by sight and god will guide me threw my battles. Since I had my soul in Christ the enemy was plotting again. Now I was running into guys who didn't accept rejection. I meet a guy named Timmy and it was a normal situation for me we talked hung out and recently here a month ago as I write this book the guy wanted more want to be in a relationship I didn't want that there is a time for single season in life and I needed to learn more self love and heal before I got into anything else serious lets just say I seen red flags in him and I knew he wasn't for me the enemy was not happy about that I told him we were cool but to go to the next step no I wasn't getting involved he acted like he understood little did I know it was the enemy thinking I was still a fool. I get up on a Saturday morning put my robe on and I hear a knock at the door I open it and its him he throws a picture of me that he drew in my house on fire I yell I no your not trying to set my house on fire my kids are in here? the door was cracked by this point I turn my back for a few seconds to put the fire out and he used that opportunity to sneak in I turn around thinking he gone I shut and lock my door I got into my room to grab my phone to call the police I walk in and hear my door close behind me in my head I was like flight mode here it goes its sad when your used to going threw abuse I was now fighting a guy who was mad that I didn't want them. So were in a tussle he takes my phone and says you better not call the police talk to me I was like no its time for you to go I gave you an option to leave the first time he wasn't trying to let me out the room I yell for my son he's upstairs and he comes downstairs and threw the door I yell call the police my son says you have my phone I'm like omg I grab his phone and I figure a way to BO guard him to slide my son his phone I crack the door and I give my son his phone the guy out powers me and starts slamming my hand in the door repeatedly I keep calm still I've been threw pain this is nothing and I didn't want my son freaking out more than he already was when you see someone hurting you on purpose its evil I snatch my hand out the door it closes now I only have one arm to fight back I tell my son go for help my son doesn't leave I hear him say Mom just get to me so I soon realized I couldn't give up the fight I had to make it on the other side if that door I had kids to get to so I start hitting him to let me out remind you I'm trying to get out and my son is trying to get in threw the grace of god I don't know how my son did it but son pulled the door off from the other side to get me I seen the door split in half as soon as it breaks the door falls hits a picture on my wall and a piece of glass has know cut my sons chest open this was getting worse by the minute they guy was standing in shock and didn't no you he came to the wrong house this was a house of warrior and we had god to help us I then see my daughter running down the stairs crying she was asleep I told her it was OK the guy tries to then charge for me again by the grace of god again I grab my son and daughter and toss them out the front door I told them to go for help keep in my mind my life wasn't important at this point there life's matter so here I was standing face to face with the enemy in my mind I'm hoping the police come soon I have very little fight left in me so he backs up and I back up like we were two bulls about to take charge I had a plan for him though he starts to charge for me I scoot back and I trip him so he falls on the floor this was my opportunity to get out I open the door and run next door were my kids were the police lady pulls up and runs in my house to see were he was the EMT had took my son because his chest was bleeding he was on the back of the ambulance my little girl had went in with my neighbors until everything was calmed down I was catching my breath something tells me to go in my house luckily I did he was now in a tussle with the female officer and I had to help her she told him to give me my phone back and he refused I yell call for back up its only us two she calls for back up and now were trying to get him on the ground glass was everywhere smoke was everywhere the door was in the middle of my hall it looked like a crime scene in my home I hear back up and its a guy I was happy they drag him outside literally too the cop car he yells don't listen to her she's been molested, she's been beat, she's crazy, he says I'll put voodoo on her and her kids, he says to me I will get your kids you won't have them I say God is my refugee and you will not do such things they put him in the car I had no time to think about what he said but the enemy wasn't done. I hear the guy cop say I see situations like this were the women don't fight or let it happen you were the Mama bear who saved her cubs I start tearing this was a level I had repeat to show the enemy I was no longer accepting any and every type of guy in my life I stood up and my self worth meant more he says your calm Neveah, I say in the Bible it says God will keep you calm in the mist of the storm he smiles and proceeds to his job. The EMT tells me my son may need four our five stitches but he couldn't go because of the Covid – 19 pandemic yes as of today not only was the covid-19 outside I was going threw this so I tell them OK I'll go to get him so liquid stitch and other items to doctor on it they say that would be good for him and they return to the truck to leave. They finally drive off with tornal in the car and they wrap up my report we are all in the house I remember telling my son not to grow up and be like him and telling my daughter not to date guys like that to forgive him and pray for him then say yes ma'am and I run to Walgreens to grab what I needed for my son I end up grabbing a sling for my finger with my adrenaline going back down I could feel my knuckle sore, my wrist sore, and my arm also sore I began praying for god to heal my son and me as well. A week goes by I hear a knock I open it and guess who there CPS (Child Protective Services) I was like here we go I hate dealing with these people again I hate this he put CPS back in my life but I wasn't worried I can't help the people I run into but I fought for my kids to make sure they weren't hurt at all. The lady that comes over slips up and says I read the report I see you were trying to make him leave I wasn't going to come out to your house my boss made me I knew then the enemy thought he was running the show I told that lady God is my refugee and no weapon formed against me shall prosper. She really had nothing to say but I had to take my son downtown for questioning my son has never been in this type of situation but I knew God would have my back funny thing is my case just closed and ruled out the enemy was trying to snoop but the more words or Christ I gave them the more it had the enemy flee because it wasn't crime for my son to stick up for me and it wasn't a crime that I was trying to save my kids instead of me. So here I am still writing this book and dealing with battles on a daily but you know who gives me my peace, my calmness, my strength God and I thank him for that. My life has been a roller coaster but I wrote this book to inspire and to help the next person for you to see and realize "When in life battling with the enemy" Remember But God".

My Conclusion

I know you're wondering what am I doing now? Well threw these battles I am proud to say I am writing this book. I am now a property manager of an apartment complex, I plan to also open a clothing store soon to sell ladies and little girls clothing. I am also still single there is season for everyone to be single this is teaching me more self love and more knowledge I need in Christ right now it's me and gods time though there are sacrifices I must make on OK with doing so because no matter what tears or battles I may have been threw the joy god has for me in the future is worth it as I look back I don't dwell on anything I look for the lessons it has taught me people think they were trying to make me fold but not realizing this only made me stronger, and wiser it made me find what my purpose was in life and that was to help others who may have been in my situation, or know of others who were in these situations and also to learn to avoid these type of situations and most of all to choose Life with Christ and not Death with the enemy. My next move will be Dallas Texas and that means in the bible (the season for meadow dwelling) which means it's the season to dwell in my blessings. I am very proud of myself and I look back at my life. It gives me chills but I know to Remember But God. I have a small support system but its OK I have Taylor witch is going to become a pastor soon I have chris moore who is a very dear friend of mine who has been with me threw most of the battles in Abilene Chris would never believe the stories I told him until I finally wrote about it it wasn't that he thought I was lien he was in disbelief how could a single mother go threw so much with no help and still remain sane in life you know what I told him Remember But God even though he was in college at Murray University in Abilene he took out time to help and listen to me when I had no one to run to and I have my dear friend terry moss who I meet. Threw chris moore he only knew my name not my story but when it was time for me to write my book he helped and coached me threw it and also learned that people complain about the small stuff in life when the person next to them have been threw a entire different level of things and others shouldn't complain at all he is also a student at ACU (Abilene Christian University) who had also wrote a book as well. As I end this chapter of my life I want you all to always pay attention to red flags in people when you see them don't give them the benefit of doubt a gut feeling is a guardian angel feeling so take it and ladies going threw abuse of any type its not right at all your self worth deserves more than that if they do it once they will do it again get out forgive pray for the person and let go and let god. Woman protect yourself your mind your energy you don't need a man to make it in life get right with god and let him lead you to the King he has that awaits for you also don't bring people to your home or around your kids unless you no this person is for the right also never put anything past a person a situation so small can easily happen because your in a comfort zone of thinking you really know these people including family members self awareness is a must battles come and go in life we all have them and have to go threw them but when you walk with the enemy your walking on thin ice for death but when you walk with God there will be battles but there will be no worries because he will help you threw each one so Dedicate your life today god doesn't care how long it takes you he will always be ready with open arms for you to receive Abundance in life. Keep up the fight no matter what you go through no matter what comes your way and Remember When in life battling with the enemy Remember But God.

Printed in the United States
by Baker & Taylor Publisher Services